Etched in Gold:

Journey back to Consciousness

Etched in Gold:

Journey back to Consciousness

By

Nonica Ganesh

Acknowledgement

I would like to thank the Divine Source, the Supreme Light that never left me, even in the darkest nights.

To my amazing children, who gave me a reason to keep rising when all I wanted to do was hide – you are my heart walking outside of my body.

To my grandmother and family members who shaped me, for better or worse – your presence taught me strength.

To the military that helped forge my resilience and courage.

To every enlightened soul or other who has crossed my path – you helped guide me closer to my truth.

Finally, to every reader who holds this book in their hands – may you feel seen and reminded that your pain has purpose, your story matters, and your light is already waiting to be remembered.

Table of Contents

Page Left Blank Intentionally

Etched in Gold:

Journey Back to Consciousness

Only by Enduring the Darkest Nights was I Able to Behold the Beauty of the Dawn.

This book is written for anyone who has walked through the fire of a dark night of the soul or faced a spiritual awakening. If you feel like you've lost yourself—it is because, in many ways, you did. And that loss was necessary. The version of you that could no longer carry your truth had to fall away. What you're experiencing is not the end. It's the unraveling that makes space for your becoming. You had to lose your old self to discover the version of you that was always waiting beneath the surface: wiser, softer, stronger, and more whole. This isn't the end of your story. This is the return—the remembrance. This is what I call the *Great Awakening*—the moment your soul begins to remember who it really is.

For so long, I believed I was simply surviving—moving through pain, confusion, and loss with no clear sense of why it all had to hurt so deeply. Each moment felt like a trial. Each day, there was a battle within me. But something greater was at work, something unseen yet ever-present, calling me to look beyond the surface. Walk beside me through the sacred unfolding of my awakening path, veiled in darkness yet guided by divine hands, leading me to the light within me and the rebirth of my soul. What I once thought was the end was only the beginning—a doorway into the truth of who I am and why I came here.

This is the story of how I remembered. This is not just a story of healing, it is a remembrance of love. Of self. Of the soul. It is the unraveling of all I thought I was, so I could become all that I truly am. I share this with you not for pity and not because I have all the answers, but because I've walked through the fire that I thought would destroy me. Instead, I found beauty within the burn. If you, too, are standing on the edge of your own, becoming—wondering if the pain you've endured had a purpose or if the darkness will never end—know this: you are not alone. There is a magnificent light waiting for you, too. And it's already inside you.

This is my story, but it's also a mirror for you. If you've ever felt like your world was falling apart, maybe it was just rearranging itself into something much higher. If you've ever questioned your worth, your path, or your purpose, I want you to know that you are not alone. You were never meant to stay asleep. You came here to wake up, to rise, to love—first yourself, then others. My prayer is that through these words you are reading, you feel seen, held, and inspired to keep walking—even when it's dark. Especially then. Because the light is not just coming, it's already here.

Chapter 1:

The Awakening Begins—An Unseen Stirring

Sometimes the greatest shifts begin in silence. What I felt that morning changed everything I thought I knew about myself.

I went to bed on Wednesday night feeling normal, but when I woke up Thursday morning, something felt off. I couldn't quite explain what was happening, but I knew with absolute certainty that something had changed. It wasn't dramatic or loud; it was subtle, but undeniable. I couldn't pinpoint whether it was a shift in my mental state, my physical body, or something even deeper, but I knew I wasn't the same as I was the day before.

The questions that echoed in my mind were, "What kind of shift is this?" "Was it energetic?" "Was something happening on a cellular level? Spiritually? Emotionally?" I had no clear answer. Outwardly, everything looked the same. I was in the same home, the same body, the same life—but inwardly, it felt like the ground had moved beneath me, and nothing was quite where I'd left it.

Everything around me seemed to suggest that all was as it should be, yet my mind and body told a different story. A quiet unease sat with me, whispering that I had crossed some invisible threshold during the night. I hadn't seen it or consciously chosen it, but I had stepped into something new.

As time passed, it became clearer: something within me had shifted between the moment I closed my eyes and the moment I opened them again. Something unseen had stirred, awakened, or returned—and it would change everything. The world that

I had seemingly known all my life had suddenly fallen from under me and vanished overnight. The security I once clung to—the sense of safety I thought was unshakable—had vanished without a trace.

I searched for it instinctively, but it was nowhere to be found. My body and mind began to rebel, resisting whatever unseen force was trying to take hold of me, fighting against the intrusion with a desperation I couldn't explain. Being mentally clear and focused was how I had grown up, so when those things became challenged, I didn't know what to do, and I began to panic until I had to pull myself together as much as possible.

Before the onset of my awakening, every day followed the same familiar pattern, a steady rhythm that offered a quiet kind of comfort. There was peace in the predictability, in knowing exactly how each moment of my morning would unfold. I knew what time to wake up, when to get dressed, when to care for my sweet pup, and when to leave the house so I could make it to work on time. Even on days when I woke up with a headache or a cold, the routine stayed the same. In many ways, I was living what I'd now call "Groundhog Days"—repetitive, uneventful, and seemingly safe. And I was okay with that. The structure gave me a sense of control, a feeling that I had a handle on my world.

But this day was different.

I woke up at my usual time, just like always, but something wasn't right. Not just emotionally, but mentally, spiritually. Something was off, and I knew it immediately. It wasn't a feeling. It was a knowing—clear and sudden. My thoughts felt muddled, as if a dense fog had settled over my mind. It was like I was here, but not fully here. I couldn't explain it, and I couldn't shake it.

I started questioning everything. *Am I losing my mind? Am I sick?* I searched for something to anchor me—some sense of clarity or familiarity that could make the experience make sense. But nothing came. The internal disorientation was so profound that I could no longer rely on the routine that once grounded me. That morning marked the quiet unraveling of the life I had once found comfort in—and the beginning of something I had yet to understand. The first thing I thought to do was conduct a survey of my home. The sofa sat in its usual spot. The television remained exactly where it belonged. Everything seemed untouched.

I moved from room to room, checking and rechecking, making sure I hadn't missed anything. Every material possession was in place, just as I had left it the night before. On the surface, everything appeared normal. My body was intact. My mind, at least physically, was intact. Yet deep inside, something was terrifyingly different, something I couldn't see but could feel tightening around me like an invisible thread. The world as I once knew was gone and nowhere to be found. To put what I was feeling plainly: Everything outside of me looked the same—it smelled the same, felt the same, and sounded the same—but nothing was truly the same. What had happened to me? I didn't have an answer, only the unsettling certainty that something unexplainable had shifted overnight. And I needed to uncover the truth.

No answers were coming, so I began to panic even more. I became terrified of not knowing what was happening. I became terrified of the unknown. I equated what I felt to drifting off while watching a lighthearted, feel-good movie, only to wake up trapped as the main character in one of the most terrifying horror films I had ever seen. Suddenly, I was mentally sprinting for my life, desperate to escape a nightmare I hadn't signed up for. But there was no exit—not yet. I couldn't just climb out of the movie screen and rewrite the script on demand. All I could do was wait for the intermission, wait for the quiet to return because my mind had become unbearably loud.

Another way to describe what I was feeling was that my mind and body felt as if I had started out on a sandy beach under a sunny sky, where everything seemed calm and predictable. Then, without warning, massive waves came crashing further and further inland, swallowing the shoreline with violence I couldn't escape. Before I could find my footing, the largest wave surged forward and catapulted me helplessly into the middle of a vast, unforgiving ocean.

One minute, I was up, gasping for breath, and the next, I was pulled under into open waters teeming with unseen dangers, an endless expanse full of the deadliest predators my mind could conjure. It wasn't just disorienting; it was the sudden, gut-wrenching realization that I was utterly alone, exposed, and fighting for survival in an ocean that had no mercy. Each predator was waiting for its turn to strike me down or for me to show a sign of weakness. It's a feeling of helplessness where no one offers support, only highlighting how vulnerable we truly are.

They were surrounding me and just waiting for the right time to take me under and into the vast darkness of the unknown. I began to believe that I was completely fighting for my life, mind, and soul. It was the battle of a lifetime, the relentless fight against my own inner darkness. There was no one there with a boat or a life vest to assist me or to save me in this battle. What I was gaining from this was survival, nothing more, nothing less. I was alone in it. I was totally and utterly alone. The darkness within me started rolling in at that time. If anyone knows anything about dissociation, that is what it mentally began to feel like for me.

The fear of the unknown gripped me, refusing to loosen its hold. It wrapped itself around my thoughts like an iron chain, tightening its grasp with every passing moment until even breathing felt like a conscious effort. I searched for answers, but all I found was silence—deep, unsettling, and impossible to escape. My mind tried to comprehend what was taking place in my real life. However, since I couldn't put an actual label on what was happening to me, a battle of the wills of my mind and soul began to take place. I began to feel out of my body, hence the dissociation.

Again, I knew what was happening all around me, but it was as if I was slowly being drowned out, and something else was taking over. That something else wanted me badly. It stalked me with eerie patience, like a predator toying with prey it knew could not escape. It felt personal, not random. It seemed like a direct attack, deliberate and cruel, and my attacker was out for blood. Not just anyone's blood. It was my blood it thirsted for, my spirit it longed to consume. It knew me intimately, better than I even knew myself, and it wanted me with a hunger that felt ancient and relentless. This wasn't fear of something unknown anymore—this was war. This felt like a hostile takeover, and I was on the battlefield.

The darkness pressed in, shaking me to my core. Suddenly, an overwhelming fear surged through me, so intense it felt like my entire body was ready to shut down beneath its weight. What made everything even more difficult was that I still had to prepare for work that day. Why couldn't it have happened on a weekend or a holiday, when I typically had time to process and ground myself? I truly believed I would've been better equipped to handle what was unfolding if it hadn't landed on a regular weekday.

But that wasn't in the cards for me on that pivotal morning. I've always believed that everything happens for a reason and in its divine timing. Still, that belief didn't make it any easier, not when I was desperate for answers that just weren't there. Nothing I had access to could explain what was happening, and no amount of searching brought immediate clarity.

Before I left for work, I remember asking my son if he had noticed anything different—if he felt a shift in the energy of the house or in the atmosphere around us. What I feared most was confirmed when he replied, "No." He hadn't felt anything unusual. And that's when I realized the truth: the shift wasn't external. It was happening within me.

I couldn't put it into words at the time. All I knew was that everything around me looked exactly as it had been the night before—but something deep inside had changed. I didn't know if I had crossed into another realm, dimension, or plane, but I was certain that my internal world had shifted in a way that hadn't yet touched the external. I was living in the same house, but everything inside me was different. As I moved through the motions of getting ready that morning, nothing felt grounded.

The internal shift didn't arrive with chaos. It came in silence—an overwhelming, echoing kind of silence. Like the stillness just before a storm, but only I could sense it. My awareness became razor-sharp. I began to notice the slightest inflections in people's voices, the tension humming quietly in the atmosphere, the unspoken weight behind even the most casual glance. Things that I never really noticed before.

It felt as if a veil had been pulled away from my perception. I wasn't just seeing with my eyes anymore—I was perceiving with my soul. And for so long, I felt it was all too much. I wasn't sure I was ready for what I was beginning to sense, to feel, to know. Well, not until months later.

My body moved, but it felt foreign, like I was watching myself from a distance, detached from the world I used to belong to. The air around me felt heavier somehow, like it was pressing in on me from all sides. My thoughts were racing, but no answers came. It was as if something deep within me had cracked open, and the light—or maybe the truth—was just beginning to leak through.

I feel energy. Deeply. Sometimes overwhelmingly. I don't just walk into a room—I naturally read it. I sense when something is off, even if no one says a word. Whether it's joy, grief, fear, or truth, I feel it in my body, my stomach, my spirit. Sometimes, it arrives as a wave of knowing. Other times, as an uneasiness, I can't quite explain. I remember walking into a room and coming close to crying, overwhelmed by someone else's emotions. I have felt anxiety creeping in simply because someone near me was anxious.

That day, I didn't know what to think. I remember feeling as if all my emotions—sadness, fear, anger, anxiety—had been tossed into a mixing bowl and set to high speed, spinning wildly out of control while the outside world remained steady, unaffected. That is the only way that I could explain away my internal state that remotely made sense. My mind and body went into a fight-or-flight mode suddenly and stayed that way for months. I still have bouts of anxiety from time to time, but that is the nature of things right now.

I couldn't shake the feeling, no matter how hard I tried. It was as if something was terribly wrong, but I couldn't quite name it. Had something happened to me overnight that I couldn't remember? Was someone I loved in trouble or hurt? Or was I picking up on a neighbor's energy? Something heavy lingered. There were no words for what I was sensing, only a deep, unsettling knowing. Something was off. That much was clear. All I knew was that whatever had a hold of me was real—and it wouldn't let me go.

I remember years ago, just before a heartbreaking event happened to my little cousin. I must have been around 16 or 17. I told my mother I couldn't shake the uneasy feeling in my legs—it was as if something heavy and unseen had settled into them. It wasn't just nerves; it felt deeper, almost ancestral. Like my spirit was sensing a storm on the horizon long before my conscious mind could understand. It was a quiet warning within, a whisper from my soul. And it wasn't just my legs. At times, without warning, my stomach would twist and tighten into knots as though it sensed an invisible shift in the atmosphere, something no one else seemed to notice.

Those moments imprinted themselves on me like silent alarms ringing deep within. Warnings I could never unhear, even if I wanted to. My mom reassured me that there was nothing to worry about, and I tried to push the feeling aside—but it lingered. That nagging sense of unease clung to me for nearly two weeks.

Then, one day, my mom mentioned we were heading over to a relative's house for a wellness check—they hadn't been answering the phone. When we arrived, we couldn't even get close to the door. Emergency vehicles were everywhere, blocking the way. Something had clearly gone wrong. We had to wait until our relative was ready to talk before we learned what had happened.

But deep down, I already knew—something beyond explanation had been warning me that a tragedy had taken place. Still, I wasn't prepared for the weight of what we were about to hear. And just like that, the nervous energy that had haunted me for weeks disappeared as if it had never existed at all. It was as if that heaviness, that gnawing unease in my body, had been a signal—one I didn't fully understand at the time.

But once the truth was revealed, the signal had done its job. My body no longer needed to sound the alarm. That moment changed something in me. I began to realize that I was deeply connected to energies, to emotions, to events that hadn't yet occurred but somehow already existed in the unseen. It was my first real brush with the intuitive side of myself—one that I would come to know intimately in the years that followed.

Reflective Questions:

1. Have you ever woken up feeling different—mentally, emotionally, or spiritually? What changed?

_____

_____

2. What did "normal" look like for you before your spiritual shift?

_____

_____

3. What part of your life gave you the illusion of control?

_____

_____

_____

4. When was the first time you questioned your reality or beliefs?

_____

_____

_____

"Even when I didn't understand what was happening, something sacred within me was awakening. I trust the stirrings of my soul—seen or unseen, I am rising."

Chapter 2:

Unseen Storm—The Dark Night of the Soul

Before I share what happened next, I need to explain a term that would later help me make sense of it all.

The Dark Night of the Soul is a term rooted in mystic tradition, often attributed to St. John of the Cross. It describes a period of intense spiritual desolation, inner turmoil, or identity crisis, where the soul feels lost, disconnected from meaning, and stripped of its previous truths. This phase is not a punishment, but a sacred initiation into deeper awakening. It often arises just before a spiritual breakthrough and is meant to dissolve the ego, illusions, and attachments so that a more aligned, authentic self can emerge. It is painful—but profoundly transformational.

What I experienced was not just anxiety, mental turmoil, and depressive symptoms. It was what I later discovered to be the Dark Night of the Soul...

I remember the morning of my initial awakening. Something deep inside of me had cracked open, and what poured out was raw, untamed, and overwhelming. My mind was flooded with questions, each one beginning with "What if..." **What if I were losing control? What if none of this was real? What if I never came back from wherever I was going?** The flood wouldn't stop. It circled me, consumed me. I couldn't silence the questions because they echoed louder than anything.

I struggled to quiet the torrent of thoughts, each one crashing into the next, while the sharpest edge of anxiety I'd ever known pressed against me. Still, I had to steady myself—there were things to do, a day to face, and work waiting beyond the chaos. After moving through my routine, the shower, the quiet motions of self-care, walking my puppy, and making sure he was set for the day, I pulled myself together as much as I could. On the outside, everything looked normal. But, on the inside, I was unraveling. Still, it was showtime. I stepped out the door like I had on so many occasions before, but this time it felt different.

The world moved around me as if nothing had changed, but everything inside of me had. I tried to trick my brain into believing everything was fine, convincing myself that nothing was wrong. But no matter how many times I repeated those words or went through my usual morning routine, it didn't help. The uneasy feeling gnawing at me only grew stronger, and with every passing minute, it became harder to ignore. The discomfort, the sense of something being off, was becoming almost unbearable.

I wanted nothing more than to retreat into the furthest corner of my bedroom closet and hide there until the storm in my mind passed. Maybe, just maybe, if I sat there long enough, I would feel better—better enough to face whatever was coming. But I knew I couldn't do that. I had responsibilities. I needed to go to the office.

Still, part of me longed to stay hidden, to shut everything out for as long as possible. Truth be told, if I had the choice, I might have stayed in that closet for months.

I decided to head to work, which was 19 miles away from my home, hoping that by the time I arrived, I'd be feeling better. But as I drove, I started to notice my vision was getting progressively worse. I blinked several times, hoping it would clear up, but nothing helped. I even tried switching to my newest pair of glasses, but I still couldn't see properly. Just days before, my vision had been perfectly fine, but now it felt like something had changed overnight. There was a strange energy—like movement in front of my eyes, and I struggled to see clearly. It felt like I was on the verge of fainting.

I had always heard of it happening to other people for one reason or another, but it had never happened to me, and honestly, I never imagined it would. It just wasn't something I thought I'd ever experience firsthand, until that day. However, on that fateful day, a deep, unsettling instinct told me that things were about to take a turn for the worse. My mind raced with the knowledge that something wasn't right, yet I also knew I couldn't afford to lose control, especially not while driving. I had to remain alert, focused, and vigilant. Every part of me was determined to stay safe, not just for my own sake, but for the other drivers around me as well.

That morning, the traffic dragged on, inch by inch; each slow-moving vehicle was a harsh reminder of how powerless I felt—trapped, frustrated, and unable to change a thing. The journey to the office seemed to go on forever, each minute stretching out, the uncertainty in my gut growing heavier with every passing second.

I remember rolling down all four windows in my car, hoping the fresh air might help, but the sound of the wind hitting my eardrums was unbearable. It made my entire body vibrate from the inside out, like a sudden chill had taken over my nervous system. I tried turning on the radio for a distraction, but even that became too much. No matter how low the volume was, the music felt like it was being screamed through me. Every word pierced my senses, and the instruments felt like someone was banging a new drum set right inside my head. It was as if my body was repelling every note, every frequency.

I couldn't take it. All I could do was focus on getting to work, one breath, one mile at a time. I turned off the radio, rolled the windows back up, and drove silently. It was one of the longest, most exhausting drives of my life. Why had I suddenly become hyper-sensitive and hyper-aware of everything around me? The night before, there were no warning signs, no obvious health issues. Yet now, my entire body felt like it was screaming for attention, though I couldn't pinpoint why. There was no physical pain.

I was mentally present, aware of my surroundings, but my mind felt clouded, as if a massive, dark thunder cloud had descended over my brain. And the thunder was deafening. Fear took hold of me like never before. It was as if I were sitting alone in the middle of a wide, open field while the fiercest storm imaginable tore through everything around me. At the time, I couldn't see that I was being held—protected—within that storm. But that understanding came later. I'll share more as the story unfolds.

I pulled into the parking garage near my job and handed the payment to the parking attendant. I couldn't bring myself to look him in the eye. Even that felt like too much. When he gave me the garage ticket, I took it carefully, deliberately avoiding any contact with his hand. The thought of absorbing someone else's energy was overwhelming. In that moment, even the smallest exchange felt like too heavy a burden to bear.

I was in deep mental distress—and energetically wide open, like a magnet to everything around me. By the time I arrived at work, I was struggling just to hold onto my own mind. And still, I had no answers, and no idea what had shifted in me between sunset and sunrise. Was it a stroke? Witchcraft? Depression? I considered every possibility, swinging between the logical and the unexplainable.

All I knew was that something was happening—and it was bigger than I could understand. I hadn't gone to bed feeling sad, angry, upset, or sick—so why was that happening to me? As I began researching, I noticed that many of the symptoms I was experiencing mirrored those of depression. But I had never dealt with depression before. I'd never experienced anxiety attacks or anything close to that level of mental and emotional turmoil, so why was it happening? Why did it all happen at once? It felt like it had come out of nowhere, with no clear trigger or warning.

I had so many questions on top of trying to act like the perfect employee at work. I had to behave as if nothing was happening to me. When someone wanted to have a conversation with me, I did my best to act like everything was fine, like I was the same person I had always been. You know, pretending to care when, in reality, I didn't give a damn about most of the work topics or the small talk that would normally fill the day. Things like, "How was your weekend?" "What did you do?" "Where did you go?" or the inevitable question, "So, who are you dating now?"

I stayed polite and cordial, going through the motions, but inside, I was wanting to be left alone. I needed space—space to think, to cry, and maybe even to scream. I desired to do all of it at once. I wanted to know why—why me?

I didn't want anyone else to experience what I was going through, but the truth was, I was terrified. Terrified of what was happening to me, and even more terrified of what was happening inside me. I felt the weight of everything pressing down, and I couldn't escape it. I smiled, made small talk, and went through the motions. No one could see or feel the storm I carried inside of me. I learned early on how to wear masks, how to function even while falling apart. But even as I played the part, something in me had shifted. I couldn't numb what I was feeling. That fear reached into the very core of my soul, leaving echoes I couldn't silence.

Was it a mental breakdown or something even worse? I was fully aware of everything happening around me. My memory was intact, my thoughts were clear, and yet...something inside me felt completely off. I couldn't make sense of what was unfolding inside my body. It didn't align with logic, and that made it even more unsettling. I wasn't losing touch with reality, but I was losing touch with a version of myself I thought I understood.

I did my best to act like everything was normal at work, like nothing was wrong. But the truth was, I wouldn't have known how to explain what was happening to me even if I tried. I was still me, but somehow...I wasn't. It felt as though something else was trying to take control of the wheel of my mind. I didn't know what it was. Was it something dark? Was it something trying to harm me? Was I losing my grip on reality...or was something bigger unfolding? My thoughts were intense, erratic, spinning in every direction. To say I was confused would be an understatement. I was in uncharted territory, grasping for understanding in a storm of mental and emotional chaos.

Every time I followed one trail, trying to make sense of what was happening, it felt like I hit a dead end, then another. It was like going down rabbit hole after rabbit hole, only to be met with brick walls instead of answers. I even began to wonder if some company I recently had over brought something dark into my home. At that point, I wasn't ruling anything out. Everything felt possible. Everything felt…off.

I suddenly recalled a well-known movie where spirits leapt from one person to the next, and a chilling thought crept in, and I couldn't help but wonder if something like that was unfolding before my eyes. Or was it something else entirely? I didn't have any answers, only fear. And fear had me in a tight grip. All I wanted was to be alone, in a dark, quiet, and safe room. No noise. No movement. Just me, myself, and whatever was left of my peace.

All I focused on was breathing. If I could keep breathing steady—just slightly different from my usual rhythm—it reminded me that I still had some control. Even the smallest sense of control was better than feeling completely lost. On top of everything, I was overwhelmed by a level of anxiety I had never experienced before. It wasn't just my own emotions. I truly believed I was feeling the emotions of everyone around me, as if I had absorbed the energy of people within a five-mile radius.

The weight of what was happening to me was unbearable. I went to the emergency room simply because I needed to feel like I was doing something. I needed answers—any explanations that I could grasp. I just wanted something that made sense. It took every ounce of willpower I had just to sit in that waiting room to be called. I felt like I could sense the energy of every single person in the hospital. Maybe that's a bit of an exaggeration, but the intensity was crushing. I was completely overwhelmed.

After what felt like hours—though it may have only been minutes—the nurse finally called my name.

She took my temperature and checked my blood pressure. She asked me what brought me in to be seen. I tried to come up with something, anything, so that they would examine me. But the truth was, I couldn't pinpoint a single thing. There wasn't one clear cause, nothing tangible that I could name.

She continued with her questions, asking things like, "How are you feeling?", "How long have you been feeling this way?" and "When did your symptoms start?" Each question seemed to dig deeper into me, and before I knew it, the floodgates opened. I started to cry uncontrollably.

Tears poured out of me, unstoppable, like a waterfall that had been building up pressure behind an invisible dam for years. The release was both overwhelming and terrifying, as though I was finally letting go of all the emotions I had been holding back, and I didn't know if I was ready to face them.

The poor nurse waited for what seemed like an hour until I was back in control of my out-of-control emotions, and then she continued with her questioning as if she hadn't seen or heard anything. I didn't know if her actions were due to a lack of interest or because my reaction was something she had seen many times before. Either way, she stayed calm, which helped me to become calm. I'm not a pretty crier either, but she never flinched.

The doctor did a full examination but found nothing physically wrong. I was sent home with more questions than I came in with—and not a single answer that brought me peace. I remember walking to my car parked across the street from the hospital when the mental fog around my brain grew even heavier. Driving home became a challenge—my vision had noticeably worsened, making the journey feel even more disorienting than before.

My eyes began picking up on even more energy or particles swirling in the air. It resembled steam rising from hot pavement on a sweltering day—except this wasn't coming from the ground. It was all around, hovering at eye level, no matter which direction I turned. I had never witnessed anything like it before.

The static-like noise in my ears, which I can only describe as white noise, had started a couple of months earlier. I never found a clear explanation for what was happening to my hearing. Even now, I still experience the ringing and that ever-present hum. Sometimes it intensifies, then settles again. I did make it home safely. I took my time, paced myself, and reminded myself that I had someone depending on me—my pup.

None of what I was going through was his fault. All he wanted was to play and eat. Looking back, I can laugh a little because caring for him gave me a sense of purpose and routine. In a time when everything felt chaotic, he was my grounding force—one small piece of normal that helped me hold it together.

There was a stillness that rose up inside of me, but not the peaceful kind. It was more like a sacred pause—a suspension between the life I once lived and the truth I was now stepping into. Every step I took that day felt like I was walking between worlds. I was still present, but part of me was somewhere else, gathering pieces of a bigger picture I couldn't yet see.

Reflective Questions:

1. What internal shifts or emotional storms have you experienced that seemed to come without warning?

_____

_____

2. In what ways have you resisted or surrendered to your own unraveling?

_____

_____

3. What did the darkness teach you about who you are beneath your roles, labels, or pain?

_____

_____

4. If your soul was trying to get your attention during a painful season, what do you think it was trying to say?

_____

_____

"Even in the darkness, I am becoming. Even in the storm, I am held. I trust what I cannot see, for the night is only a passage—and I am walking myself home."

Chapter 3:

Spiritual Attacks—When the Veil Thins

What if the fear you felt in the dark wasn't just in your mind? I faced forces that couldn't be seen—but their presence was undeniable.

Beyond the veil of my blurred vision and clouded thoughts, mysterious nocturnal events began to unfold, emerging from the shadows without warning or explanation. Let's talk about the nighttime terror spiritual attacks—experiences I can only describe as otherworldly, even interdimensional. They always came at night, right as I was about to fall asleep. I'd get settled, close my eyes, and just as I began to drift off, the disturbances would begin.

At first, it was subtle: strange, unfamiliar sounds. But those noises would quickly escalate, growing more intense and aggressive, as if something unseen was trying to breach the veil between worlds.

The attacks continued night after night for months. I had experienced nightmares before, but nothing like that. What I began facing was far more intense—more vivid, more relentless—than anything I had ever known. They happened so frequently that I began to expect them, so much that fear slowly faded…I remember times when I would finally relax enough to fall asleep, then out of nowhere, something would strike the bottoms of my feet. Other times, I'd feel sudden bumps against the bed or hear loud, jarring noises erupting out of nowhere. Without fail, it would jolt me awake, pulling me right back into that unsettling awareness.

These attacks felt like something far beyond the ordinary—supernatural, even. They were personal. Deeply personal. It was as if I had done something to anger someone—or something in the spirit world, something that made me an easy target for the kind of relentless assault I was experiencing.

The attacks came in waves, stretching over several months, and they didn't just feel random. They felt calculated, as if they were designed to chip away at me, at my very core. At the time, I was in a state of emotional turmoil, vibrating at such a low frequency that everything seemed clouded by sadness, fear, and confusion. My awareness and mindset were so far removed from peace, from strength, that I couldn't even comprehend the extent of the toll those attacks were taking.

Each invisible attacker seemed to feed off my vulnerability, making me feel smaller, weaker, and less in control. It was like I was trapped in an endless cycle of negativity, unable to break free.

I dug through endless information, searching for answers—until I finally stumbled upon something that resonated deeply with what I was experiencing: the Dark Night of the Soul.

It became clear to me that this was Divinely guided. I had sifted through countless resources and watched video after video—any of which could have made sense—but none resonated the way the concept of the Dark Night of the Soul did. I had never heard of anything like it before. But I know without a doubt that it was my Divine Source, my Guardian Angels, Ancestors, and Guides—perhaps all of them placed that Dark Night of the Soul video in front of me at exactly the right moment. Call it what you will, but it was no coincidence.

Prior to that video, suffocating darkness had surrounded me, relentlessly trying to drag me further into the depths of an unseen abyss, consuming every thought I had. I poured every ounce of myself into trying to make sense of what was happening, but the harder I tried, the deeper I sank. It felt like I was slipping into a pit of something nameless, faceless, and unfamiliar. I didn't know if I was meant to pass through it or if it would swallow me whole. Fear gripped me—fear of what was happening, fear of what might come next. When you let the unknown consume you, it can be paralyzing, and I let it rule me for months.

Something was pulling at me. It was unseen to the naked eye, yet unmistakably real. It felt like a vortex, a powerful force that knew my name and latched onto every part of me— my mind, body, and soul. It wouldn't release me. I clung to myself with everything I had. I fought with every fiber of my being—for my sanity, for my soul, for my survival.

The darkness pressed down on me like a heavy weight pinning me to the ground while life itself hovered like a referee, ready to count me out. It might sound dramatic, I know, but it was real. I knew in the depths of me that a power greater than that darkness existed. I believed in that light. But at that moment, I couldn't find it.

I searched every corner of my mind. I combed through my heart. I called on my will to rise. But the light, the strength, the presence I was looking for felt just out of reach. The struggle was exhausting. It was like being caught in a rip current, trying to swim back toward a safe shore, where peace waited. But the more I swam, the more the undertow of darkness dragged me deeper into its cold, churning waters. I was desperate to feel my feet on solid ground again. But just as I tried to rise, my ego stepped in and intervened—an invisible force pressing down with its own heavy weight. It became yet another burden

I had to carry. It whispered doubts into my mind, telling me I was losing control, that I couldn't overcome what I was facing. But it was lying.

Then, one night, my Higher Power gave me a dream that revealed something I had never encountered before: cognitive dissonance. It's the concept of holding two opposing beliefs at the same time. These weren't words I typically used— truthfully, I'd never considered them before. But in that moment, something within me clicked, and a much-needed light switched on, bringing clarity where there had only been confusion.

I began to see that my ego was pushing me to believe one thing, when in fact, what was happening to me was something far more profound than I could have ever explained or imagined.

I couldn't explain the darkness I was in, so my mind tried its best to fill in the blanks for me, but if it weren't for my Higher Power providing me with those two words, I would have believed the ego. The ego only knows what it has already been through, so it will trick you if you let it.

The moment I stopped dismissing the invisible and the moment I started listening to the truth that lived beneath the surface of things was when my transformation began to take root. I know I have already said a lot, but I must now go back to the beginning of my life so you can get a clearer understanding of my story, of what I believe led me to such a devastating and dark place, and then to the most amazing and transformative discovery of my life and self, one I could never have dreamed possible.

Reflective Questions?

1. Have you ever experienced unsettling dreams or nighttime disturbances that felt spiritual or energetic in nature?

_____

_____

2. Do you feel there are energies or forces beyond the physical world that have interacted with you?

_____

_____

3. How do you protect your energy or spiritual space during vulnerable times?

_____

_____

4. What role do you believe fears play in spiritual growth?

_____

_____

"I am divinely shielded and deeply rooted. No force, seen or unseen, can shake my truth. Even when the veil thins, I stand in sacred protection. Light surrounds me, and nothing not meant for me may enter."

Protective Prayer: *"I now call upon the Highest Light and Divine Protection. Wrap me in a shield of love, truth, and sovereignty. I release all fear, all foreign energy, all illusions of danger. My spirit is whole. My soul is ancient. My will is strong. No force of shadow can enter where the light of truth resides. I walk in faith, not fear. I walk in clarity, not confusion. I stand rooted to the Earth, connected to the Heavens. I claim my peace. I claim my power. I claim my light. And so, it is."*

Chapter 4:

The Darkness that Shaped Me

Our first wounds don't just leave scars; they shape how we see love, safety, and ourselves. This chapter holds the weight of my first breaking.

I was three years old, barely old enough to understand the world around me, when I received my first and only spanking from my father. At the time, I didn't realize how deeply this would imprint on my sense of safety and worth. I don't remember the exact crime that earned me that punishment, but knowing how some three-year-olds can behave during their infamous "terrible twos and threes," I'm certain I must have deserved it.

What I do remember, with crystal clarity, is the tool he used: a brightly colored afro pick comb—the kind that men proudly wore in their hair back in the early 70s, a style statement that made them look effortlessly cool. In that moment, though, it wasn't cool—it was a symbol of discipline.

I don't remember the spanking hurting, at least not physically. The thin, plastic prongs of the comb probably didn't leave much of a sting. But what hurt the most—what burned itself into my memory—was the fact that it was my father's hand, guided by his decision, that delivered it. It wasn't the pain of the spanking itself, but the sting of knowing I had disappointed him.

It was a moment that marked me in a way I didn't fully understand at the time—when love, discipline, and the weight of parental authority collided. Even at that young age, I sensed that it wasn't easy for him either. That tiny, colorful comb became more than a tool of correction; it became a symbol of a lesson, one I would carry with me far beyond my toddler years.

After that spanking, my dad walked out of the apartment that my mom and I lived in, unaware that it would be the last time I'd see him until I was sixteen years old. During those missing years, my dad was in and out of prison. He wasn't a bad man; he was kind and soft-hearted, but he struggled with drug addiction and kept company with people who didn't lead the most upright lives.

I was primarily raised by my mother, who, for as long as I can remember, battled alcoholism and exhibited strong narcissistic traits. She wasn't a gentle person—or quiet alcoholic either—her words were sharp, and her actions were often too harsh for a young child growing up around her. When she drank, everyone around her felt the impact of her anger and volatility.

One of my male cousins once said that my mom was one of the toughest uncles he had. I chuckle at that statement now, because it holds some truth to it. To say my life has been turbulent would be putting it mildly; it's been a storm of trials, survival, and resilience.

For now, I'll keep this at a surface level, as what I am about to share offers important context for the path that eventually led me to uncover who I truly am. I once heard that some of us choose the lives we're given before we arrive here. If that's true, and if you identify as someone who came to serve a greater purpose, then you'll inevitably face battles meant to shape you. These challenges aren't just for your own growth, but so you can help guide others through theirs, because people naturally gravitate toward those who truly understand them, who can listen without judgment, and offer compassion instead of criticism.

I will mention my mother frequently because of the profound impact she had on my life. But before I share those stories, I want to be clear: I was never without the basics. I never had to worry about a roof over my head or the availability of warm water to bathe in. Whether it was in a clean, modest home she maintained herself or under the care of a family member in her absence, my mother always ensured I had my basic needs met.

That stability was a blessing in itself—a foundation that many children are not fortunate enough to have. And while my mother's journey and choices left their mark on me, it's important to recognize the determination she poured into ensuring I never went without the essentials.

As I mentioned, I was sixteen when I saw my father again after all those years. He had finally been released from prison and came to live with my mom and me. I was overwhelmed with joy and relieved to have him back in my life. I needed him for so long. I needed him to rescue me, to be the anchor I had longed for. At the same time, I remember him feeling like a stranger to me. A stranger that I met a lifetime ago. It was a confusing and conflicting state to be filled with both deep longing and unfamiliarity. Still, I was overjoyed by his return.

I remember running through the house like an excited little kid the day he came home, filled with a childlike silliness I hadn't felt in a long time. I believe it was just a day after his release from prison when I allowed myself to believe that the mysterious figure I'd long known as my dad had finally come home. I truly thought he would stay—that he'd be with us for good. My naïve mind wanted so much to believe that he would never leave me again. After all, I needed him so much.

But my dad stayed with us for approximately three days before he gave up and moved out. I believe the pressure of stepping into the role of a full-time father, combined with the challenges of living with my mom, was simply too much, too soon.

My dad went on to live his life and eventually got married to a lady whom I didn't know. My mom had mentioned her before, but I had never actually seen her until one day, while driving with my uncle, we spotted them walking down a narrow street in our small town. I recognized my dad's walk instantly. I asked my uncle to slow down so I could say something to them. But when I spoke, neither of them looked our way. We were right beside them, just a few feet from where they were walking on the sidewalk, yet it was as if we or I were invisible.

I remember calling out, "Dad! Dad!" and then more urgently, "DAD!" I even called him by his birth name, but he never turned to look my way. It was as if my voice couldn't reach him, no matter how loud I became. I must have looked like a cartoon character—the kind that screams so wide and loud you can actually see their tonsils vibrating. (HA!)

There wasn't any tension or stress on his face; it seemed like I was yelling through a mirror at my dad, but only I was able to hear. The echo was so loud and painful. It was as if every time I yelled "Dad," the word itself would ricochet off the mirrors that I was seemingly encased in, become pointed, and stab me in my heart repeatedly. I can feel the pain to this day, and it has been years since that incident. The saddest part of the whole thing was that I had my whole torso literally hanging out of the car window while waving and waiting to be acknowledged by my dad, and I received nothing back.

That day, he offered me silence. And that silence carved a lasting wound that shaped decades of my life. If I had gotten some type of acknowledgement that day, I believe that my life would have turned out differently. Not good or bad, just different.

The silence spoke louder than any words ever could.

My uncle tried to comfort me by saying things like, "Be strong. Don't let it affect you." He was right—at least in theory. Maybe I should have just flipped the switch and made an excuse not to feel. But I couldn't. I couldn't close off my emotions. I had already weathered so much emotional turmoil in my young life, but turning off my feelings wasn't an option. I felt everything—every ache, every sting of rejection.

I always wore my heart on my sleeve (as they say), and whatever I felt, you could see it in my eyes. After that, I truly felt that I was nothing. My young heart had been through so many heartbreaks over the years, but that day, my heart broke into a billion pieces, it seemed. I tried to be strong in front of my uncle, but I remember my heart crying.

Reflective Questions:

1. What part of your identity had to be stripped away in your darkest hour?

_____

_____

2. What helped you keep going when everything inside you wanted to give up?

_____

_____

3. Has silence ever become too loud for you? If so, what did you do to overcome it?

_____

_____

4. Have you ever experienced disappointment from someone you trusted? How did you respond, and what did that moment teach you about yourself and others?

_____

_____

"Even in the shadows, I was becoming. What tried to break me only carved me into clarity. I am not what I survived—I am who I rose to become because of it."

Chapter 5:

Chasing Echoes—Running
After the Ghost that Wouldn't Stay

Sometimes we chase love not for what it is, but for what we hoped it would heal in us. This was the beginning of that chase for me.

The emptiness my father left behind that day carved out a hollow space in me—a space only a father's presence could have filled. Paired with the emotional wounds my mother inflicted, it set me on a path of longing. I craved love. I ached for happiness. I just wanted to feel whole. I just wanted to feel like I mattered in this world, but all the world ever seemed to do was remind me that I didn't. I mattered to no one, I felt. And in time, that silence echoed so loudly, I stopped mattering to myself.

Growing up, there was a silent ache and a yearning inside of me that I couldn't name. It felt like I was always reaching for something warm, steady, and safe in the men I chose, but it was never truly there. It was as if I were chasing a shadow of what the little girl in me longed for: Protection, attention, unconditional love. But instead, I kept finding absences wrapped in temporary affection. That unmet need followed me quietly, shaping my choices, whispering in the background that maybe if I tried harder, loved deeper, or hurt more silently, I'd finally be enough to make someone stay.

I began chasing my father's affection in the arms of men because somewhere deep down, it felt like that was what I was meant to do—like love had to be earned, proven, or found in the same kind of absence I grew up with.

If the men chased me back, it didn't feel right—almost foreign. My egoic mind was wired for pain, for absence, for longing. Love that came freely felt unfamiliar, like it couldn't be trusted. I knew how to chase well. Chasing was second nature to me; it was all I knew. It never even occurred to me that I wasn't supposed to. Looking back, I wasn't pursuing real love—I was desperately chasing a ghost, an echo, the idea of the father who had left me on read.

The men I chased did exactly what they were meant to do— they ran. Looking back, they mirrored the abandonment I hadn't yet healed, reflecting the very wound I was unknowingly trying to fix through them. I believed the chase was love. I thought the feeling of not being good enough was simply part of the equation. Without realizing it, I let the pain of my earliest experiences with my parents shape my definition of love and self-worth.

I thought that feeling of being "not good enough" or "not desirable enough" was a part of love. I let those early interactions between my mom, my dad, and me shape that belief. They became the lens through which I saw myself— always chasing, never feeling worthy of being caught.

I was in so much pain that I barely recognized its presence. Not the kind that fades after a fall, but a relentless ache—one that clung to me no matter where I went, who I spoke to, or what I did. It was always there, shadowing every moment. It lurked constantly, as if waiting to see whether I'd find a vice to soothe the ache inside. I had an ache that could not be soothed at that time, not by anything or anyone. The ache was ever-present in my daily life.

As I recall, prior to my awakening, I couldn't remember ever being truly happy. I looked over the photos that I had taken over the years, and I recalled that all my childhood photos told the same story. I saw a fake or forced smile, and the saddest eyes. I remember seeing clowns with smiles that could light up a room, and with the saddest eyes that could darken that same room. That was me in a nutshell.

To speak about my dad again, there was one moment, about a year or so after he had ignored me, that left a lasting imprint as well, but not enough to reverse the damage that had been done to my heart. He showed up unannounced at my grandmother's house, where I was still living at the time. My uncle and I were getting ready to head to a teen club to celebrate the incoming new year. My dad quietly came inside while I was caught up in getting dressed, and for a while, I forgot he was there.

He was always soft-spoken, calm in his presence. At some point, someone made a comment that drew my attention to my dad, who was sitting in a corner chair at the time. When I looked his way, he was already watching me.

There was warmth in his eyes I hadn't seen before—so much pride, so much love. I had recently graduated from high school, and at that moment, I felt seen. It was the look I had craved my entire young life. I only wish he had given me that look before my young heart began to shut down.

If I'm honest, I'm still searching for that look today, in the eyes of a man who will see me the way I've always needed to be seen. That look was priceless.

My dad has passed away, but I will never forget him. I wish we could have been a better father and daughter duo, but that's okay now. Thank you, Dad, for that look! Maybe that is what your purpose was, and for that, I am forever grateful.

Reflective Questions:

1. What early experiences or relationships shaped your belief about what love is and how it should feel? (Did you eternalize love as something you had to chase, prove, or earn?)

   _____

   _____

2. Have you ever found yourself pursuing someone who remained emotionally unavailable? (What did that experience reveal about your inner needs or unresolved wounds?)

   _____

   _____

3. In what ways have you mistaken emotional intensity for love, and how has that impacted your self-worth or sense of identity?

   _____

   _____

4. What part of yourself were you really searching for in the people who kept leaving—and how can you begin to offer that to yourself now?

   _____

   _____

"I no longer chase what was never mine to hold. I turn inward, where my love has always lived. I am enough. I am home."

Chapter 6:

The Move—When Home Chose to Let Me Go

Some places release us before we're ready. This is the story of when home became a memory, and I was asked to find shelter within myself.

I moved in with my grandmother immediately after my mother came home drunk from a party and threatened me with a weapon, saying that not only was she going to hurt me, but she would also hurt herself, too. I remember her coming into my bedroom, waking me up from my sleep. She was talking, but I was still groggy from being awakened long after midnight. I remember her pointing at me with what I thought was her finger. Her internal rage was quiet yet explosive, and at that moment, I no longer felt safe under her roof. Fear surged through me like it never had done before. I was stunned, frozen, but most of all, I was heartbroken.

My mom was the one who should've been my shield, but instead, she became the storm. The one who was meant to guard me from harm was the one who wanted to harm me the deepest, far beyond the damage already done. After I ran to a different part of the house, she told me to pack what little clothing I had and to leave immediately. I prepared to leave as quickly as I could, carrying my shattered sense of safety.

She made me call a taxi at 2 a.m. I had no money, so I had to rely on the hope that my grandmother would be home to pay for the taxi. My grandmother always worked the night shifts as a nurse, so I was unsure whether she'd be home at that time.

Someone was watching over me because she was indeed home and was able to pay for the taxi. What my grandmother said to me that night made me realize that she was aware of how my mom was treating me, but she likely felt she couldn't do anything.

My grandmother's words were, "Did your mom kick you out of the house?" I said yes, and she told me to come into her room to sleep. I felt safe there. She did what she could to ease my aching heart, and I am forever grateful for that.

About a week before everything exploded, I had asked my mom if she would take me to my childhood boyfriend's boot camp graduation. She said no, but when I asked if it would be all right for me to go if I found another ride, she agreed. His mother was kind enough to offer me a seat in their car. It was going to be a long trip—eight or nine hours each way—but I was excited and grateful.

There were no cell phones back then, just payphones, and our journey was tight. We barely stopped, not even for food or restrooms. They actually packed drinks and sandwiches, so we wouldn't have to stop for food. We stopped for gas once going and once returning. I was totally at the mercy of his family's schedule. When I returned home, the first thing my mom said wasn't "Welcome back" or "I am happy you made it safely." It was, "Why didn't you call me?" I explained honestly that we hadn't stopped, and I hadn't had the opportunity. But she didn't want honesty. She wanted a target. Her anger escalated quickly.

She began calling me names, then, out of nowhere, she threw an entire can of beer at me. It hit the window, bounced, and landed near me. I calmly picked it up and placed it on the TV stand, stunned and unsure of what had just happened. I walked to my room in silence, trying not to cause any more problems. Everything was quiet until she came home drunk, filled with whatever darkness that had been brewing inside of her.

My grandmother saved my life in more ways than I can count. Her love, her strength, and her prayers wrapped around me like a shield. Even now, I believe her prayers still linger—protecting, guiding, and holding me through storms. When my world felt too cruel, too loud, too unstable, she was my safe place. Her quiet strength, her undeniable love, and her unwavering prayers she sent up on my behalf still wrap around me like armor. She gave me a chance to breathe, to heal, and to begin rebuilding some of the broken pieces of myself—pieces that I didn't even know were shattered.

Even now, long after her voice has faded from this world, I am so grateful to her. I believe her prayers never stopped; they still echo beyond time and space, surrounding me like whispers from the Divine. They remind me that I was never alone. That even in my darkest nights, someone saw me. Someone believed me, and someone believed in me. And sometimes, that's all it takes to change a world.

Reflective Questions:

1. When someone or something you called "home" rejected you, how did it shape your sense of self-worth?

_____

_____

2. What emotions did you have to suppress in order to survive that moment, and have you revisited them since?

_____

_____

3. In what ways did that forced transition teach you strength you didn't know you had?

_____

_____

4. What does "home" mean to you now, and how can you create that space within yourself?

_____

_____

"Even when I was cast out, I carried home within me. I am no longer seeking shelter—I am the sanctuary."

Chapter 7:

The Military—Fighting One
War to Escape Another

*They say structure builds strength—but sometimes,
structure is where we go to hide. The military became both
a battlefield and an escape.*

I enlisted in the military just three days before my 19th birthday. It felt like a bold leap into adulthood—I was finally claiming something for myself. But beneath that rush was a quiet mix of excitement and nerves. The thought of starting a new chapter was thrilling. I had never truly been on my own; the longest I'd ever been away from family I'd known all my life was a short two-week stretch.

Now, I was about to leave everything familiar behind—the chaos, the comfort, the dysfunction, the known. I told myself I was ready, but part of me was just running, praying that freedom would feel like peace. Joining the military brought a shift I wasn't used to—I couldn't just leave when things got hard, so I adapted to a temporary reality that, while challenging, became strangely easy to adjust to. Basic training came with strict rules, and one of them was limiting our freedom to shop. We were only allowed to buy essential items a couple of times during the entire training period. So, all my checks were quietly deposited into my bank account, untouched.

That same pattern continued when I transitioned straight from basic training into military schooling. Shopping privileges were still restricted, only granted during a certain phase closer to graduation. Week after week, my checks kept flowing into my account. I hadn't been able to check my balance the entire time, so I daydreamed about what it would look like. In my teenage mind, anything over $500 was a fortune.

The day finally came when I was allowed to go out on my own—a milestone that felt like true freedom. I was proud. The trainees had to walk everywhere, but I didn't care. I was ready to see the fruits of my labor and maybe treat myself to a small shopping spree before graduating. I practically skipped to the ATM, excited to see how much I had saved since leaving home. Before the military, I worked in fast food for minimum wage. So, this felt like a big step forward— a sign I was finally getting somewhere.

When I finally reached the ATM, I was eager to see the results of all the work I put in—months of early mornings, late nights, and physical and emotional endurance. I planned to withdraw a small amount to celebrate a little. But when the screen displayed $200, my heart sank. I stared at the number. There had to be a mistake. I couldn't believe that was all that I had after everything I had been through. After the initial shock wore off, I called my mom to ask what happened to the money I had worked so hard to earn—money that came from my blood, sweat, and literal tears. But before my fingers dialed her number, I remembered something important: when I opened the account two years earlier, she had been added to it. At the time, I was a minor, so I had to add her to the account. Now, that detail felt like another betrayal from the one who was supposed to protect me.

That moment unlocked something I had forgotten—my mom had access to my account. She had taken everything I had earned, leaving only $200 behind. And what made matters worse, I had just received orders to deploy to Germany in a couple of weeks. I was preparing to travel across the world with barely any money to my name. Before leaving, I had to purchase necessities that quickly ate away at what little money I had left. By the time I landed in Germany, I had $20 in my pocket. I remember calling my mom, not just to ask, but to plead for an explanation. Her response pierced through me like a blade: "Well, I needed the money." No remorse. No apology. Just those five words—cold, detached, and deeply wounding.

I was still just a teenager, barely out of high school, and she was in her thirties, young, healthy, and vibrant. She could have worked. She had options, but she chose other avenues. That money was supposed to represent my independence, struggle, and sacrifice. And just like that, it was gone. This was another time that I felt all alone. I had to parent myself. I was so angry. But underneath all of it was grief. And deeper still was a hollow kind of resolve: I would survive this. Even if no one showed up for me, I would show up for myself.

Am I still bitter that my mom nearly emptied my bank account? Honestly, yes, a little. Because moments like that don't just vanish, they plant something in you. They shift your story. That moment triggered a cycle in me—a deep, unconscious belief that maybe I wasn't meant to have money. Maybe I didn't deserve it.

That memory pulled up another one—another lesson etched into my spirit far too young. I was working at a well-known fast-food chain. After weeks of saving, I proudly told my mom that I had $312 in my account. For a teenager, that was a big deal. Something inside me hesitated before sharing it—an instinct, maybe—but I ignored it. She was still my mom. I wanted her to be proud of me.

About a week later, I was one of two employees opening the restaurant on a weekend. It was around eight o'clock in the morning when I saw her. My mom came walking up to the drive-through window, banging on the window to get my attention. I was stunned as she had never done that before. Confused, I opened the window and asked what she was doing there. Without hesitation—and loud enough for my co-worker to hear—she said, "I need to borrow $300 to get my friends out of jail. I'll pay you back." In that moment, I knew that I would never get that money back. I gave her the money, not out of trust, but out of obligation. I felt small, used, and helpless. And I still had to get through the shift. I wanted to cry, but I couldn't. I had to keep going.

The accumulation of moments like that—especially in a young life—can completely change the way you see the world. It can twist your perspective on what it means to live fully, financially, emotionally, and spiritually. And spiritually? That's the hardest part to name. Because sometimes, when the people closest to you betray your trust, it doesn't just hurt—it makes you question everything. It makes you wonder if you've been forsaken. If maybe there's no safety anywhere.

But I've come to realize that feeling, as real as it seems, isn't the truth. Life is going to hand us moments that break us wide open. The choice we get to make is whether we let those moments define us or refine us. We can stay stuck in the story of what was done to us. Or we can rise, scarred but stronger, and say: "This will not be the end of my story." At some point, we all must decide—will we let what hurt us become who we are, or will we put on our big-girl or big-boy pants, dig in, and move forward? I choose forward.

Reflective Questions:

1. Have you ever tried to escape something, and did you find the freedom you were looking for?

_____

_____

2. What parts of yourself had to go into hiding to survive a certain chapter in your life?

_____

_____

3. When you went into hiding, how did it shape your view of control, safety, and personal identity?

_____

_____

4. When you escaped, did you feel protected and relieved, or did you continue to suppress your inner world?

_____

_____

"I fought battles no one could see—and I survived them all. My path may have been forged through struggle, but I now walk in strength, purpose, and truth."

Chapter 8:

First Duty Station—Alone but Still Standing

You don't know how strong you are until solitude wraps around you like a second skin. Germany was where I learned what loneliness really meant.

After completing both basic training and military schooling, I received orders for my first duty station—Germany. I remember feeling incredibly alone. Even though I often felt misunderstood by my family, like I didn't quite belong, I was rarely alone—they were always around in some way. The only consistent absences were my mom and dad.

My grandmother had eleven children, and my mother was the oldest of them all. My youngest uncle was only about three years older than me, so we spent a lot of time together. We hung out at parks, skating rinks, restaurants, and even worked side by side at the fast-food place I mentioned earlier. My uncle was the other heartbeat of my youth. He was the one who felt like home when nothing else did. We were inseparable, like two peas in a pod. Everyone thought we were siblings for the longest time. If he was near, I was not far behind, unless we were working or in school. His presence softened the sting of a world that often misunderstood me.

When I landed in Germany, that familiar warmth was gone. I arrived carrying a quiet ache that pulsed beneath my skin. I felt like the loneliest girl in the world—displaced, uprooted, and barely holding on. What little foundation I had crumbled, and I was reaching blindly, for something steady. Something like love. Or what I thought was love. I only knew I wanted to feel something, anything that reminded me that I was still alive.

Soon after settling in, I went on a few dates. Then I met him—a man so striking. But red flags fluttered like storm warnings on our first date. I saw them, but I chose to overlook them. I was tired of empty spaces. Tired of waiting for someone to choose me. I mistook attention for affection, and chemistry for connection. I mistook beauty for safety. I didn't love him. I loved the idea that someone might finally see me.

Everything in me resisted him. I didn't like his scent—it felt unfamiliar and wrong. I didn't like his friends, the way they moved through the world with arrogance and recklessness. I didn't like the way he'd manufacture arguments, just to disappear and leave me sitting in silence. He was beautiful, but everything else in me said no. And still, I stayed because I hadn't yet learned that wholeness could be found in my own arms. That I was the one I had been waiting for all along. What made it more difficult was that the first time we were intimate, I already knew deep down that I didn't truly like him—not really, not at all.

There were no sparks or fizzles. There was no connection, just a moment of misplaced hope wrapped in need. And as fate would have it, I became pregnant from that encounter. Soon after, the truth began to unravel little by little. I learned he had feelings for a young woman back in his home state—the same woman he claimed never existed. He told me he wasn't seeing anyone, wasn't talking to anyone else. And I, wanting to believe him, took his word without question. I knew he was a flirt, but I hadn't realized the extent of his dishonesty.

One day, I found it—a congratulatory card shaped like a baby's bottle tucked among his personal belongings. It had words scribbled inside like "Congratulations" and "Thanks for telling me." When I asked about it, he brushed it off like it was nothing, and I tried to let it go. I told myself not to be the jealous girlfriend, not to make waves, even as my instincts whispered the truth.

I was so excited about my baby. But when it came to her father, there was no joy, only disappointment and quiet dread. I was carrying a life I already loved with my whole heart, but the man who was tied to that life brought me no peace. To be fair to him, he wasn't a terrible man, but every part of my soul, every silent scream within me, urged me to run. To walk away. To leave him behind. We dated a year before he asked me to marry him.

I still remember the proposal not because it was beautiful, but because of what came after. He casually confessed that one of the only reasons he proposed was because his uncle told him, "You might as well marry her; you already have a child together." It wasn't love that led him to ask. It was an obligation. And deep down, I knew it. Looking back, I can see the quiet ache I carried—how deeply I wanted love to bloom where only duty was planted. I mistook proximity for partnership and presence for love.

I thought having a family would heal what had been broken in me or calm the storm that was residing deep within the walls of my being. But I was searching for someone to choose me, not out of responsibility, but out of genuine love, reverence, and desire. I now understand that love cannot be borrowed from someone else's expectations. It must be chosen freely, fully, and without pressure. What I was really seeking wasn't a ring, a title, or a promise made in haste.

I was longing to be seen…really seen. And that kind of recognition can't be faked, forced, or handed down through advice from an uncle, friend, or anyone else. It must rise from truth. And I hadn't yet learned how to choose myself first.

Not once did I ever truly consider marrying him—not until he asked, and I mistook the obligation for fate. We planned to wed in another European country, a picturesque escape dressed up as a beginning. The ceremony came and went in a blur—a fragile performance, paper-thin. Afterwards, we wandered the cobblestone streets of a small, storybook town, but there was no fairytale waiting for me there.

It wasn't long before the insults began—sharp, familiar, echoing like warnings I had ignored. I walked beside him as a wife, but inside, I wept as a stranger to my own choice. When he wasn't looking, tears rolled down my face, not from surprise, but from the bitter confirmation that I had married a mistake I had felt in the marrow of my bones.

He and I went through countless ups and downs, including several separations. Looking back, we were a terrible match. Still, I wanted another child—I wanted to have two. Two years into our marriage, I asked if we could have another, and he agreed. I didn't care why he said yes; I was simply happy that he did. That moment felt like it locked me into the marriage. At that point, I stopped caring about the relationship itself. I had my children, and they became my focus.

I poured everything into trying to give them the life I never had—love, attention, toys, conversations, all of it. Focusing on them helped me survive the emotional turmoil. Pain had become such a constant that I barely recognized it anymore. I blame myself because I could have walked away long before I finally gathered the strength to leave for good. I had become so numb that I forgot what pain even felt like, until it would suddenly hit me out of nowhere. When the weight became too much to bear, I buried the pain so deeply within myself that I convinced my heart that nothing could ever reach me again. That cycle repeated itself repeatedly until it couldn't.

Now, I can clearly say that my children's father was a narcissist. I always sensed something dark in him—the way he looked at me sometimes, or how his face would appear almost ghoulish in sleep, like something out of a horror movie. Over time, it became clear he was a master manipulator, and I had been his puppet for years. I didn't realize the extent of it until I overheard him telling our daughter, "I can easily manipulate your mom; all I have to do is make her think it was her idea." That sentence stuck with me. After that, I started questioning everything he said, and eventually, we separated for good.

How could someone be so cruel? I wish I had recognized the signs sooner, but I didn't, because I don't think in those terms. Reflecting on our relationship—the gaslighting, name-calling, cheating, emotional rollercoaster, constant blame—it's amazing I didn't go down with the ship. Even though I knew I didn't belong in that relationship, he kept finding ways to break my heart, repeatedly. Eventually, I couldn't feel my heart anymore. There seemed to be an empty space where it used to be. All I felt was pain, disappointment, and the endless cycle of chasing something that wasn't real.

I remember the pressure I'd constantly feel at the crown of my head. Stress, fear, and sadness were constant companions. Over time, I believed I didn't deserve anything good. Even the relationships I had after him might have felt physically satisfying, but deep down, I knew those people weren't good for me. And the ones who were kind, emotionally present, and genuinely wanted to know me? I self-sabotaged every time. They never stood a chance because their emotional availability felt foreign, almost wrong. I was used to pain, and in a twisted way, it felt more comfortable than kindness.

Self-sabotage became a habit. Whenever something good came into my life, I found a way to ruin it, convincing myself that people didn't like me or that they were somehow flawed. In truth, it wasn't them, it was me. I entered relationships I had no business being in. I hurt good people who didn't deserve it. That was never my intention, but it happened. To anyone I've hurt along the way, please accept my deepest apology.

Today, my relationship with my children's father is cordial. We speak occasionally without any hostility on my part. What matters most to me now is that I left that relationship with my dignity intact—and I am truly grateful for that.

Reflective Questions:

1. When have you found yourself in a new environment where you felt completely alone? How did that isolation impact your sense of identity and self-worth?

_____

_____

2. What coping mechanisms did you develop (or wish you had) to stay grounded during times of drastic change or unfamiliar surroundings?

_____

_____

3. What strengths within yourself helped you survive (or still help you survive) when everything around you felt foreign, uncertain, or overwhelming?

_____

_____

4. Have you ever mistaken a relationship or connection as a remedy for your pain or loneliness? What did that reveal to you about your inner needs?

_____

_____

"Even in the unknown, I did not fold. Though I stood alone, I stood tall. I carried the weight of my past and still showed up for my future. I am proud of the strength I found along the way."

Chapter 9:

Soul on Fire—The Chase That Broke Me Open

He wasn't just a person—he was the match that ignited everything buried. What began as a desire, turned into the fire that burned me clean.

I met a man online, someone I found attractive, but not the kind of man I would normally take a second glance at. That's not to put him down or elevate myself. We all have preferences, and honestly, he didn't check all my usual boxes. He was tall and slim, and while I may have noticed his height, there wasn't much else in his photo that stood out to me.

He messaged me first. It took me two days to respond. I don't even remember why I hesitated, but I do remember hovering over the "send" button after typing a simple reply to his hello. I paused, and then—somehow—the message was sent. After that, I kept scrolling through other messages, not thinking much of it, but he responded almost immediately.

We ended up talking on the phone, and soon after, we agreed to meet up for a late lunch at a casual restaurant chain. I arrived first, even though I had told him I was running late, and he replied that he was too. I waited about ten minutes before I saw a tall, slim man who was limping slightly get out of a vehicle. He had told me he was tall, but I wasn't sure of his true height until I saw him. Some men tend to add inches when speaking of their height. But he was truthful.

He was easily over six feet. We greeted each other and went inside. Standing in line, I remember thinking I wasn't really interested. I wasn't feeling any kind of spark, but then he started talking, and I started laughing. Like, really laughing. It had been so long since I had laughed like that with a man. His stories, his voice, and his humor disarmed me.

In my last relationship, laughter had been scarce. There were moments, but mostly there was silence and loneliness. But here I was, smiling and laughing freely. As we talked more, I started to really look at him. And the more I looked, the more I saw how attractive he truly was. When we got our food and sat down, the first thing he did was reach for my hand and say a prayer before we ate. His hand was soft, but still masculine—just how you'd want a man's hand to feel. That simple act—the prayer—hooked my attention. Then we started talking deeply. We shared similar views on life, faith, and the world. It felt easy and aligned.

We talked for a couple of hours, and when we decided to leave, he walked me to my car. He leaned in to kiss me, but I turned my cheek toward him. I was trying to heal and evolve into the woman I was meant to be. So, he kissed me there instead, softly.

Even though I enjoyed our time, I wasn't sold yet. I felt no lightning bolts. No fireworks. In fact, I felt nothing…until he asked for a hug. That hug…that was the moment everything changed. When he wrapped his arms around me, it was like I had come home. My whole being lit up. It felt ancient and familiar. That hug activated something in me. Suddenly, everything about him made sense. I didn't know it then, but that hug marked the beginning of a journey that would completely unravel me—and awaken me. We texted a bit after that and eventually met again for another casual date.

He picked me up, and we went to eat and talked more. Again, at the end of the evening, he tried to kiss me, and this time, he got the side of my lips. It wasn't unpleasant. I just really wanted to take things slow. I was trying to do it right. After he left, I was met with silence. Three days passed without a word. I texted him saying that it didn't seem like he was interested, and I'd leave things there. He replied with the usual, "It's not like that, but I understand."

Still, I couldn't stop thinking about him.

Two weeks passed, and I tried to forget him. I tried to be logical. But I ached. I missed someone I barely knew. I didn't understand what was happening to me. I'd loved before, I'd chased before, but I had always been able to walk away. Not with him. He was sweet, intriguing, kind, and gentle, but it was something deeper that had me drawn to him.

I eventually reached out again and invited him over. We picked up pizza, tried to watch a movie, but I couldn't focus. It was him. Something that I had always unknowingly longed for. Something different than anything I had ever experienced. Something I had forgotten. He felt like me but in another body.

After we settled down, we sat on the couch, and he asked, "How would you treat me if I were yours?"

I said, "Like a king."

He smiled and said he'd treat me like a queen. Then he added, "I'm kind of liking you a little."

He napped for a bit with me beside him, and I just let myself enjoy the moment—the nearness, the stillness. But soon after…he disappeared—again. I reached out, needing clarity. The insecure side of me couldn't just let it go. I asked why he had gone quiet again. He said he didn't want to get hurt. I tried to reassure him. I told him I wasn't like the women from his past. But nothing I said seemed to reach him.

Eventually, he told me he wasn't ready for a relationship, but he wanted me in his life. We all know what that means. And yet, I didn't care. My soul cried out for him. I asked if he would cook for me one night, not for the food—though that was a bonus—but because I just wanted to be near him again. He made salmon and asparagus. The salmon was divine. The asparagus, not so much—chewy like old gum—but who cared? After we ate and ended the evening, he vanished again. Longer this time. I didn't chase in the physical sense—no constant texts, no showing up—but my mind was consumed.

Obsession doesn't always look loud. Sometimes it's just a quiet torment. I'd think about him all day, and then I would dream about him at night. I couldn't shut it off. This man hadn't done much to maintain my interest, and yet, I couldn't let go. I had fallen into a spiral that I didn't understand. And then came the research: twin flames, soulmates, soul ties, contracts. I still don't know what label fitted us. But I knew what I felt for him was not normal. It was otherworldly. And it broke me open in ways nothing else had.

He triggered every unhealed piece of me. All my wounds. All my insecurities. But through that, something in me started to shift. I descended into the darkest place I've ever known— but that darkness became the soil. I was the seed.

And from that place, I grew.

I had to be buried by pain, watered by longing, and scorched by truth in order to bloom. The love I thought I had for him was really the fire that burned everything false away—and what was left was me. Whole. Awake. On fire, not for him. But for my own soul.

Reflective Questions:

1. Was there someone whose presence or absence triggered a deep unraveling in your life? What did their role awaken within you—grief, purpose, abandonment wounds, or something else?

_____

_____

_____

2. Do you believe your connection with this person was destined, karmic, or chosen on a soul level? If so, what do you feel the soul contract was designed to teach you?

_____

_____

_____

3. How did this relationship mirror parts of you that were unhealed, hidden, or longing to be seen? In what ways were they a reflection of your shadow or your light?

_____

_____

_____

4. Have you reached a place of peace or gratitude for what that connection unearthed, even if it caused deep pain?

What have you learned about yourself through their presence in your life (or their departure)?

_____

_____

_____

"What burned me did not destroy me—it revealed me. I now see that the ache was a mirror, reflecting back the love I needed to give myself. I am no longer chasing ghosts—I am calling my soul home."

Sacred Pause: When Love Breaks You Open

Some connections don't come to stay; they come to *ignite*. This man didn't stay. He didn't offer consistency, or commitment, or even clarity. And yet, his presence unearthed something sacred within me. Not because of who he was, but because of what I had forgotten I was. This was not just heartbreak, this was initiation. Initiation into deeper self-worth. Into my inner truth. Into the kind of soul recognition that doesn't end in a fairytale, but in a fierce rebirth.

I learned that:

- *Not everyone who awakens your heart is meant to hold it.*
- *Obsession is often grief with nowhere to go.*
- *Longing isn't always about them—it's your soul calling you back to yourself.*

Through the ache, I found my voice. Through the silence, I found my strength. Through the craving for his presence, I remembered the power of *mine*. I used to think healing meant forgetting. Now I know healing is remembering who you are, even after someone couldn't see you. So, if you're reading this and you're chasing closure, clarity, or someone who can't meet you, take a breath. Come home to yourself.

*You are not hard to love.

*You are not too much.

*You are not unworthy.

You are a soul on fire—and anyone who cannot rise with you was never meant to carry your flame.

Chapter 10:

The Night Before the Storm— A Soul on the Edge

You can only push pain down for so long. The night before everything broke, I could feel something inside me start to rise.

The night before everything unraveled, before I woke in that terrifying, altered state, was eerily quiet. It was the stillness before the storm. I remember scrolling through social media, searching for any sign of the one I believed to be my twin flame—my soulmate.

My heart, still tethered to invisible threads, pulled me toward his profile and anyone connected to him. That's when I stumbled upon a photo from what looked like a family gathering. It wasn't even a clear picture of him, just a pair of slim, athletic legs in a familiar stance beside a woman, whom I presumed to be his child's mother. I laugh a little now at how sure I was, recognizing someone by their posture. But there was no mistaking it.

The person who posted the photo was related to his child's mother, so it made sense that she was there, too. Then I noticed something else. She had changed her last name to include his. Likely remarried. Still, my thoughts weren't malicious. I've never been one to wish ill or speak poorly of others without cause. What I did feel, though, was the familiar ache—the weight of unspoken emotions rising in my belly. And as always, I pushed them down.

I went to bed, burying the feelings like I had done for years—a habit formed in childhood. My mother once told me I had no feelings, and from that moment on, I learned to silence them.

When I felt afraid to speak my truth, I pushed it down.

When I didn't want to seem needy, I pushed it down.

When I felt desperate, lonely, or forgotten, I pushed it all deep into myself.

I thought I was being strong. But eventually, there comes a time when your soul says, "Enough." When no more pain can be stuffed into the shadows, when your higher self sits you down and refuses to let you run anymore, that's what the "incident" was for me—a reckoning.

Everything I had hidden rose to the surface like a tidal wave: childhood pain, unprocessed grief, years of feeling unseen and unheard. The sadness. The anger. The fear. I didn't even know I was angry until it came crashing out of me. Sometimes I'd be driving, and my chest would seize with unexplained pain, sometimes physical, but mostly emotional. My body had become the vault for decades of silence, and now it was cracking open.

I cried when I saw a deer. I cried when I passed a homeless man. I cried when I saw a line of baby ducks crossing the street. I had trained myself not to feel too deeply. Life, to me, was simple: things lived, and things died. There was no space for grief or tenderness. But now? Now I understand differently.

Everything lives on.

People. Animals. Energy.

We don't disappear—we shift. We return to the unseen realms.

I've come to understand that every creation with a soul is connected. The sadness in a stranger's eyes, the silent suffering of an animal—I see it now. I feel it. They say the eyes are windows to the soul, and I believe it. If you look closely, you can see the whole spectrum of human experience reflected there.

The truth is, we forget. We forget that everything matters. That we are part of everything, and everything is part of us. If we lived from that truth—if we stopped numbing ourselves and started feeling again—we might just heal ourselves, and each other. We were never meant to do this alone. We are always stronger together.

Reflective Questions:

1. What emotions were you most afraid to feel, and why did you believe you had to bury them to survive? (Was it grief, longing, anger, rejection, fear, abandonment, or something even deeper?)

_____

_____

_____

2. How did denying your truth begin to manifest in your body, mind, or energy field? Were there any signs prior to your incident?

_____

_____

_____

3. What did you believe would happen if you allowed yourself to fully feel what you were avoiding? (Did you fear losing control, being judged, or falling apart?)

_____

_____

_____

4. Was it a breakdown or a breakthrough? Did clarity emerge after the eruption?

_____

_____

_____

"Even in the silence before the breaking, I was being prepared. My soul felt the shift long before my mind understood. I trust the wisdom in my stillness. What felt like falling apart was really the beginning of my rising."

Chapter 11:

The Darkness—Stillness in the Storm of My Soul

This wasn't just emotional pain—it was a storm that swallowed me whole. But in the stillness, I found the first sparks of my strength.

The darkness I endured wasn't just the absence of light, it was the suffocating fog of confusion, sadness, fear, and everything in between. It clung to me for months before I could even begin to summon the strength to pull myself from its grip. I didn't know if I'd survive it. It was all-consuming. Each day felt like walking through a haunted maze. Fear and uncertainty pulsed through me like a current—there was no rest, neither day nor night.

I didn't understand what was happening inside me. All I wanted was to sleep. I wanted to close my eyes and escape. It felt like my entire world had collapsed overnight. I had awoken in a state of mental quicksand, slowly sinking. The more I struggled, the heavier the pull. Some days offered a flicker of clarity. Others felt like I was only at the beginning of a never-ending descent. I searched for answers. I came across information about depression, and though some of the symptoms aligned, it didn't feel like that. It was deeper. Darker. This felt like something ancient and spiritual, like something with a name I hadn't learned yet, or maybe I had forgotten.

Still, I fought.

Every second.

Every heartbeat.

I fought to keep my mind from shattering, to hold together the fragments of who I once was. It was like something I couldn't name had turned on me. Something dark. Vengeful. It didn't just want to torment me—it wanted to consume me.

I kept asking, "Why me? What did I do?" I've made mistakes, sure. But I'm a good person, or at least I try to be. Yet this darkness didn't seem to care about any of that. It had one target: me. And the only time I felt even a hint of peace was at night, which also became the time spiritual attacks began. Whether it was spiritual warfare or a battle within myself, I couldn't say for sure. But the war was real. My ego tried to help in the only way it knew how—through logic. It whispered possible explanations, all of them laced with fear. The ego doesn't dream. It only knows what it's been taught. And in times like those, it defaults to survival, not transformation.

I was drowning in confusion when I stumbled across a video titled "The Dark Night of the Soul." Divine intervention, nothing else could explain it. I had never searched for it. Never heard of it. But there it was, on a platform driven by algorithms. It was as if the Universe made sure that the message reached me.

And that message cracked open a truth I desperately needed: I wasn't alone. What I was experiencing had a name. It was known. And others had made it through. I remembered something similar years earlier, after my grandmother died. I had felt foggy, detached, as if I were in my body and yet floating outside of it, observing everything through glass. But that passed quickly and quietly. This time was different. This was a storm that would not move until I did. I learned that the only way through the dark night of the soul... is through it.

There's no shortcut. No numbing your way out.

The more I avoided facing my pain—both past and present—the longer I stayed stuck in the darkness. But where do you even begin when your pain goes all the way back to the beginning of your life? I started there. Maybe that's why it lasted so long—there was so much buried within me that needed to rise for healing. I anchored myself in the present, the only way I knew how—through logic, through structure. One plus one equals two. Two plus two equals four. I played brain-training games. I read. I researched. I watched video after video. Anything to keep my mind from unraveling.

I needed proof I wasn't losing touch with reality. I revisited past memories to check for gaps, to make sure my mind was still mine. And then one night, I saw another video months later—one that gently told me to let go. To stop holding on so tightly. To stop trying to control every thought.

The message was clear.

The thoughts didn't help. They were harming. The grip I had on my mind was hurting me more than helping me. So that night, for the first time, I released it. I let my body relax. I let my mind soften. I stopped fighting. And something shifted. That night became the first night I truly began to heal. Not just survive but heal. The pressure in my head, the mental weight I had carried for so long, slowly began to lift. Not overnight, but over time.

The fog remained for a while, but I could feel the difference when I really started going within. I lost physical weight, yes, but the emotional heaviness was lifting as well. That was the most profound release of all. You don't realize how much you've been carrying until it's gone.

And that's when the ego tried to claw back in, telling me this new lightness felt wrong, unfamiliar, unsafe. I had grown so used to the heaviness, the pain, that peace felt like a threat. But I refused to go back. I had come too far.

So, I kept walking.

I kept choosing light.

I kept choosing myself.

Eventually, the lightness began to feel good. Natural. Like something I could live with. Like something I deserved. I had broken free from a mental prison I didn't even know I was in. For the first time in my life, I could breathe again. And this time, I was truly alive.

Reflective Questions?

1. In the heart of your pain, what parts of you kept choosing to survive even when you felt like giving up? (What voice, memory, or flicker of light reminded you that you still had a purpose?)

---

2. What did you learn about yourself in the stillness, when there was nothing left to distract you from your own truth? (Were you stronger, more intuitive, more worthy than you ever gave yourself credit for?)

---

3. How did your ego try to protect you, and how did you learn when to gently set it aside? (What thoughts or patterns did you see that were rooted in fear, not freedom?)

---

4. What did choosing yourself truly look like amid darkness? (Was it rest, boundaries, saying no, letting go of something or someone, or speaking up?)

_____

_____

_____

"In the deepest dark, I found my own light. In the silence of the storm, I heard my soul speak. I faced what tried to break me—and I chose me. I am no longer afraid of the dark. I now carry the calm within it."

Chapter 12:

Spiritual Journey—The Sacred Unraveling

I didn't choose this unraveling. But within the anxiety, isolation, and spiritual confusion, something sacred was being born.

Just as I began to feel like I could breathe again, another video found its way to me—this time, about spiritual awakening. It was yet another term I had never heard before. But something in me leaned in.

Looking back, I realized I was already questioning my religious and political beliefs even before the dark night of the soul began, not out of sadness, but because I felt like everything I had ever been told was a lie. Lies that had woven themselves into the fabric of my identity, both physical and spiritual. One reason my dark night may have felt so unbearable was because I no longer knew who—or what—to call on for help. I was questioning everything I once believed. That sense of spiritual isolation cut deep. I didn't want to see or talk to anyone. I wanted to sit alone in the dark and disappear.

Even with that kind of isolation and a level of anxiety that could've crushed ten people, somehow, I was still given the grace to keep going. It was unimaginably difficult, but I did what I could to survive. After those initial waves of darkness, I noticed something strange: the world looked the same, but everything felt different. It was as if someone had removed a veil from my eyes. The sun still shone, the moon still rose, but nothing felt normal anymore.

There's no easy way to explain what happened next. My mind and body rebelled against everything I was sensing. It kept me in a heightened, anxious state for months. I didn't feel safe—not in my skin, not in the world. It felt like I'd been dropped into an alternate reality. One that looked like the life I knew, but felt like something I'd never encountered. Just the word "dimension" used to sound strange to me. Yet now, it was the only way to describe what I was experiencing.

The strangest part was that everyone around me seemed untouched. People carried on as if the world hadn't shifted, as if they hadn't just awakened in a new reality. I found myself thinking, if I had to wake up, why hasn't everyone else? But I came to accept that not everyone wakes up at the same time—or at all.

The world became too loud, too much. I was hyper-aware of everything. I had to push myself just to take my pup for walks. Even then, I had to pretend everything was okay. My only solace was the park, where it was quiet and empty. I was terrified to be around people, except for close family. My safe place became the dim corners of my home. One night, the anxiety hit me like a wave from nowhere. It was unbearable. I had the sense that I was picking up on energy that wasn't mine. Moments later, a family member came downstairs, visibly upset. There it is, I thought. I wasn't imagining things—I was feeling everything, even if it wasn't mine to carry.

At work, in a 10-story building, I felt as though I could sense everyone's emotions simultaneously. One day, during a training session, I nearly broke down in tears because I felt someone else's heartbreak in the room. I longed to talk to someone, anyone, who might understand. But every time I tried to explain, I could see it in their eyes: they didn't get it. They couldn't. And so, I held it all in.

Eventually, I came across more people talking about spiritual awakening. The phrase was becoming more mainstream, but no one seemed to describe it the way I was living it. That's why I'm sharing this: for anyone going through something similar, you're not alone. There's no single path through a spiritual awakening or dark night of the soul. I believe the tools and support you need will appear—if you can just hold on long enough. I still don't have all the answers. But I do know this: on the other side of my deepest pain, something sacred was waiting for me.

My awakening might've been triggered by years of buried trauma, a soul contract, or maybe it was time for me to wake up. Maybe I had reached the end of my soul's contract with unconscious living. Whatever the catalyst, I am grateful. Because before this awakening, I was numb. I was functioning—caring for my family, working, keeping up with responsibilities—but there was no joy in my heart. I think my heart had completely started to shut down. I didn't even realize it until everything inside me was shaken awake.

The awakening broke me. It shattered everything I thought I knew. But I believe that was the point. I had been sleepwalking through life, just going through the motions. My Higher Power decided it was time for me to wake up, and when that moment came, it was loud, terrifying, and undeniable.

Some spiritual teachers say we sign contracts before we're born—agreements about the timing and nature of our awakening. Maybe I had signed mine too, and when the time came, I was pulled out of spiritual sleep with no warning. I had gone so far off course that maybe a gentle nudge wouldn't have worked. I needed something seismic. Whatever the reason, I'm deeply grateful.

Yes, it was horrifying. But it saved my life. Before, I was living a lie. I had become who everyone expected me to be. I was playing roles, wearing masks. I was everyone, and yet...I was no one until I was found.

This path isn't easy. It strips you down to nothing. You purge old beliefs—generational teachings, outdated traditions—things you didn't even realize had taken root in you. My awakening required me to let go of inherited trauma and fear-based conditioning that had lived in my bloodline for generations. It forced me to question things I had once believed were sacred, even if they didn't sit right with me anymore. And I'm still in that process. Some days, I still wrestle with what my soul knows versus what my mind was taught. But I'm learning to loosen my grip. I've embraced grounding, meditation, inner child work, long baths, and mindfulness practices that keep me rooted in the present.

There was no escape from the dark night or the awakening—I had no choice but to walk through it. But now, I know that the light I was seeking wasn't outside of me. It was buried beneath everything I had been taught to believe. And now that I've found even a glimpse of that light, I'll never go back.

Reflective Questions:

1. When your anxiety was at its highest, what was your soul trying to get you to notice? (Was there a deeper truth beneath the racing thoughts that needed to be felt or seen?)

_____

_____

_____

2. How did isolation both challenge you and also protect you or prepare you during this sacred unraveling?

_____

_____

_____

3. What moments or signs made you realize that your senses were heightened (and that you were no longer experiencing life the same way)?

_____

_____

_____

4. How did not understanding what was happening to you become a part of your initiation into something greater? (Did confusion lead to surrender? Did fear invite faith?)

"Even as I unravel, I am not lost. In the stillness, I continue to grow. I choose peace now. I choose myself—fully, fiercely, and without apology."

Chapter 13:

Etched in Gold: Raised Above the World—Marked by the Divine

A dream carried me above the city and painted me in light. This chapter is about purpose, destiny, and the gold that now lives inside me.

The Meaning Behind "*Etched in Gold*"

The title was inspired by one of many vivid, lucid dreams that began to appear seemingly out of nowhere. In one dream, my Higher Power lifted both me and a male figure high above a city. As we hovered in the sky, golden outlines began to trace our bodies and the city's skyline. The dream felt deeply symbolic and intuitive, like a divine message.

Deep within, I believe I have a unique purpose—a mission that is part of something far more expansive than I can fully understand right now. Though I don't entirely understand or, as I prefer to say, "innerstand" the journey I'm on, I believe with all my heart that each of us comes to this earth with a purpose. Sometimes, we're meant to play key roles in someone else's mission, just as others will play pivotal parts in ours.

In that golden outline I saw, there were two figures—myself and another—which leads me to believe I will eventually meet or walk with someone whose path aligns with mine. There's a constant, almost magnetic pull I feel—perhaps toward that shared mission. Because of that, I'm learning to surrender to the guidance of the Highest and my spiritual protection team, so I don't try to force or control outcomes that require divine timing and alignment.

When I don't know what my purpose is exactly, I can grow impatient. But I'm learning that patience is part of the process. Everything unfolds in divine timing. Whenever I've tried to move ahead of guidance or take matters into my own hands, the result has never aligned with the highest good. So now, I choose to listen. I choose trust.

Before my awakening, I was living in what I can only describe as a slumbering world. My life revolved around work, responsibilities, stress, arguments, and self-doubt. I kept myself so busy that I rarely stopped to reflect on the deeper questions, like why I'm here, or what my soul truly came to do. But when I was forced to rest—when life sat me down—I began to awaken to truths and knowledge that I hadn't previously imagined. Insights came to me out of nowhere. It was then that I realized how long I had been asleep—mentally, spiritually, and emotionally.

The saddest part is that we are born with the truth already inside of us, but it's quickly dimmed or silenced. The powers that govern this realm understand how revolutionary it would be if every soul woke up to their true essence, purpose, and power. That's why so many systems are built to keep us distracted, divided, and disconnected. Many are still caught in that dream state. But I also believe that more and more people are awakening each day.

So many have forgotten who they truly are and what they came here to do. I believe we live in a system designed to keep us in a low vibration—to keep us stuck in fear, self-doubt, and survival mode. This kind of conditioning keeps people from even considering that there's something greater happening, something deeply spiritual and powerful beneath the surface of everyday life. The lies run deep. The betrayal runs deeper. People are taught fear over faith—taught that punishment awaits them if they don't follow rigid doctrine, or that they're not worthy unless they meet impossible standards.

Then there's the media, constantly spreading messages of fear, division, hatred, and destruction. The physical world consumes people, and they forget that they are spiritual beings on an earthly mission. We are part of something so much bigger, a profound, interconnected system of divine intelligence. We are one of the greatest creations ever made. We are life itself. And if more people truly remembered that, I believe the world would overflow with more love, more compassion, and more unity than ever before.

Reflective Questions:

1. Have you ever had a dream, vision, or inner knowing that felt like guidance?

_____

_____

2. What do you feel your soul came here to do?

_____

_____

3. What does "Etched in Gold" mean to you personally?

_____

_____

4. Do you believe your life has a sacred mission or calling? How do you honor it daily?

_____

_____

"I am etched in gold, not by accident, but by destiny. I am Divinely guided, chosen, and protected. My life holds purpose beyond what I can yet see. I rise above the noise of the world, grounded in truth, crowned in light."

Chapter 14:

Journey Back to Consciousness— The Long Walk Home

Waking up isn't peaceful—it's disruptive, disorienting, and painful. But eventually, each step brings you closer to truth.

Consciousness is more than simply being awake; it's about becoming aware in the truest sense of the word. My awakening has been one of the most intense and challenging experiences of my life. It hasn't been all peace and light. It has tested my limits, shaken my mental foundation, and made me question everything I thought I knew. It's a journey that pushes you to confront not only the world around you but your beliefs, your Higher Power, and even your sense of self. At first, nothing makes sense. Then suddenly—everything does.

Before my awakening, I found myself in a place of spiritual uncertainty. I often reached out to family members who were more spiritually connected, asking endless questions that seemed to come to me from nowhere. I questioned everything: what I'd learned in school, in church, from the streets, even what I believed about the universe. I wasn't sure if I was losing my mind or finally finding my truth. Asking questions helped. It made the unraveling easier. Because to awaken, we must dare to question everything we've ever been taught. We are living in an age of information and misinformation. While there's a flood of deceptive content out there, there's also an abundance of uplifting truth waiting to guide those who seek it.

I often think about our ancestors, who didn't have the same accesses to information as we do today. They passed down what they were taught, believing it to be true. They couldn't compare perspectives like we can today. They did what they knew, and for that, I hold no judgment. As children, many of us were conditioned to believe that adults had all the answers. We were taught not to question authority. But as I grew older, I learned that wasn't always true. Much of what was handed down through generations, whether through family, culture, or institutions, was rooted in misinformation, sometimes intentionally designed to mislead and suppress.

If I could speak to my ancestors now, I would say: "You did the best you could with what you had, and it's okay. We're finding our way back."

Healing while awakening is one of the most complex emotional experiences you can have. There are days when pretending to be still asleep is easier than trying to explain what you've come to see and feel. Some people choose to stay in slumber, not out of ignorance, but out of comfort.

There's a quote that says something like, "It's easier to accept a comforting lie than a painful truth." I may be paraphrasing, but the point stands. It's easier to stay asleep, but that sleep comes at a cost. Awakening feels less like a gentle emergence and more like a complete deconstruction. It's not some cozy cocoon where you quietly evolve into a butterfly. It's more like being thrown into a storm—a storm of confusion, grief, anxiety, anger. There are moments when you'll feel like you're losing your mind. The dark night of the soul can feel like a breakdown, but in reality, it's a breaking open.

The ego—the identity you built to survive—gets asked to step aside, and it doesn't go quietly. It resists like a stubborn child. Mine still tries to pull me back at times, but I've learned to override it and to guide it gently into alignment with who I'm becoming.

The dark night feels like an endless tunnel—until one day, you wake up, wipe your eyes, and ask, "How long have I been asleep?" For those of us who've walked through this shadowy initiation, everything looks the same on the outside, but we're not the same on the inside. The people around us haven't changed, but we have. And that changes everything.

Awakening rewires your entire being. It opens you to truths you couldn't have grasped before. Some souls were called to awaken during this time, for a reason, for a purpose. If you're reading this and resonating, chances are you're one of them. Your purpose may not look like anyone else's. It could be as simple as being a light in someone's life, or it could be something much larger. Only you, your Higher Power, and your spiritual team can define that mission. But know this: your presence here is not an accident. You have a divine assignment. In due time, it will become clear. My hope for you is that you listen, that you trust the pull, and that you rise to meet it—not just for yourself, but for the good of us all.

Reflective Questions:

1. What outdated beliefs, cultural norms, or generational teachings have you begun to release?

_____

_____

2. How has your definition of "consciousness" evolved?

_____

_____

3. How do you balance spiritual awareness with everyday life?

_____

_____

4. In what ways have you noticed yourself becoming more present?

_____

_____

"With every step, I return to myself. I walk through the shadows, but I do not walk alone. My soul remembers the way—and with each breath, I rise closer to truth, to clarity, to home."

Chapter 15:

The Transformation—Rewired by Fire

The fire didn't just burn—it rewired my mind and spirit. I emerged changed, knowing I could never return to the person I once was.

The idea of losing yourself can feel terrifying, but what waits on the other side is a clarity so profound, it feels like being reborn in fire. The mental and spiritual awareness that follows is not just awakening—it's electrifying. As I've said before, I'm not sure if it's fair or unfair to be chosen for awakening. What I do know is this: once you've awakened, there's no returning to who you used to be. You can't unsee the truth. You can't unknow what's been revealed. Life no longer feels the same because you are no longer the same.

Before, my days ran on autopilot. I'd wake up, go through the same motions, and think the same thoughts. Now, while my physical routine hasn't changed drastically, my inner world has been completely transformed. My mindset, my emotional compass, my sense of purpose, it's all shifted in a new direction.

Before my awakening, I wanted to be kind to people because I knew firsthand how painful life could feel growing up. I didn't want anyone to carry the weight I once did. Now, that kindness comes from a deeper understanding: that every single soul on this earth is carrying something unseen. Every person is walking their own path through light and shadow, and so, I strive to move with compassion, not blindly, but consciously. I do what I can to uplift, to help, to be a safe space where needed. And just as importantly, I'm learning to step aside when I can't help, honoring the space others may need to grow through their own fire.

Reflective Questions:

1. What parts of your identity have you had to release to step into a truer version of yourself? Were you afraid to let them go? Why or why not?

_____

_____

2. Have you ever gone through a situation that felt like it broke you down but it was setting you up for transformation? What clarity came on the other side?

_____

_____

3. Now that you're in the process of being "rewired," what new values, truths, or visions guide your life that didn't before?

_____

_____

4. What brings your spirit peace, and how can you cultivate more of that in your daily life?

_____

_____

"I was not broken; I was being remade. The fire did not destroy me; it refined me. I rise from the ashes of who I was, reborn in clarity, strength, and sacred truth."

In Closing:

The Awakening Continues

This transformation has been unlike anything I could have imagined. Some days, it feels as though I've drifted into an entirely new reality. Other days, I feel as if I've just awakened from the deepest sleep. When I was "asleep," all I could feel was pain. Now, I carry a lightness I never thought was possible. I'm deeply grateful for everything I've endured because without it, I wouldn't be returning to the truth of who I am.

I was created with intention. And now, I have awakened that intention. I am a healer. I am a guide. I am a teacher. On some level, I always sensed there was something extraordinary within me, but now, I know. And while the word "*grateful*" may seem simple, it holds a vastness that words cannot fully express. I am forever Grateful for my life before the awakening, and even more so for the gift of waking up to the Divine light within me.

I didn't know what I needed until the moment it found me. Someone once said, "The brightest version of ourselves orchestrates the darkest nights of our lives." I believe that. Sometimes this world feels heavy, like my soul was once at home with the Divine, but now it has been sent down here, into a realm of distortion, pain, separation, and illusion. When my soul arrived, it went into shock. Even now, part of me still misses a home I can't quite remember, a place my human mind can't describe. But I feel it. I know it.

And even with that longing, I've come to understand something vital: I'm here on purpose. And while I'm here, I choose to help. When I witness someone's eyes light up from the smallest act of kindness, it brings peace to my soul. I don't do it for a reward—I do it because I know what it's like to walk in the dark. I sometimes wish that every person could rediscover that spark and never let it go dim again.

This world has weighed so many of us down. We've become buried in the burdens of work, bills, responsibilities, and distractions, so much so that we've forgotten how to truly live. I believe this forgetting was not accidental, but intentional, courtesy of a system designed to keep us asleep to our true nature and power. But now is the time to wake up. To remember that we were never meant to live in misery, confusion, or separation. We were meant to be. We were meant to shine.

Many of us were programmed from birth to fit into roles we never chose—to play small, stay quiet, follow systems that were never designed to support our liberation. Girls were taught to play house. Boys were taught to be providers. Generations are growing up to be tired, overworked, and unfulfilled. It wasn't their fault. Many did the best they could with what they were taught. But now, we have access to a new understanding. And with awareness comes responsibility. We must begin to ask ourselves, "Why?"

Why do I believe what I believe?

Why do I feel the way I feel?

Why do I continue to repeat patterns that don't serve my highest self?

We must unlearn to remember. Heal to awaken. Question to become free. There are forces in place that thrive on keeping us divided, distracted, and disempowered. But the moment we remember who we truly are, that power begins to dissolve. The most revolutionary thing we can do now is to rise in love, in truth, and in unity. We are powerful beyond measure—not when we dominate, but when we come together in compassion, humility, and purpose. We can change this world by being kind. By uplifting. By modeling a new way of being for the next generation. By sharing the truth we've reclaimed.

Everything I've shared here is based on my lived experience and beliefs. I understand some may disagree, and that's okay. We're all on different parts of our path. Some are meant to awaken now, some later, and some perhaps not in this lifetime. But none of us is above or beneath one another. We are all divine threads in a greater tapestry.

Thank you for reading my story. If even one person feels seen, understood, or inspired by these words, then I have fulfilled part of my mission. When your awakening comes—because it will—don't resist it. Don't fear it. Let it wash over you. Let it break you open and bring you home. Go inward. Heal deeply. Because the more you heal yourself, the more healing you offer to this world.

May your soul remember what it came here to do. May your heart soften enough to heal and grow strong enough to love again—fully, freely. May you no longer run from the storms within you, but meet them as sacred messengers calling you home. May every tear you've shed become a seed for the garden you're meant to bloom in. May you trust the unraveling, honor the stillness, and rise, again and again, rooted in truth, crowned in light. You are never alone. You are always guided. And you are always—Divinely becoming.

With love,

May peace, light, and clarity guide your path.

Xoxo

About the Author

Nonica Ganesh is a veteran, writer, and spiritual guide who has walked through the fire of adversity to reclaim her truth. From a turbulent childhood to military service, her life has been shaped by resilience, deep reflection, and the quest to understand why we are here.

Her debut book, Etched in Gold: Journey Back to Consciousness, is both a memoir and a spiritual roadmap – a testament that even the deepest wounds can become gateways to transformation.

When she isn't writing, Nonica is passionate about helping others awaken to their own light, sharing tools for healing, empowerment, and self-discovery. She currently lives in the U.S. with her family, her beloved pup. She has a heart devoted to guiding others toward freedom and wholeness. She currently lives in the U.S. with her family and her beloved pup.